ANNALISA EWALD

Being at Woodstock

What It Was Really Like

Copyright © 2022 by Annalisa Ewald

All rights reserved. No part of this publication may be reproduced, stored or transmitted in any form or by any means, electronic, mechanical, photocopying, recording, scanning, or otherwise without written permission from the publisher. It is illegal to copy this book, post it to a website, or distribute it by any other means without permission.

Annalisa Ewald asserts the moral right to be identified as the author of this work.

Annalisa Ewald has no responsibility for the persistence or accuracy of URLs for external or third-party Internet Websites referred to in this publication and does not guarantee that any content on such Websites is, or will remain, accurate or appropriate.

Designations used by companies to distinguish their products are often claimed as trademarks. All brand names and product names used in this book and on its cover are trade names, service marks, trademarks and registered trademarks of their respective owners. The publishers and the book are not associated with any product or vendor mentioned in this book. None of the companies referenced within the book have endorsed the book.

First edition

This book was professionally typeset on Reedsy.
Find out more at reedsy.com

Contents

1

Introduction

The Woodstock Music and Art Fair, billed as *An Aquarian Exposition,* really was "three days of peace, love and music" as advertised. Epic and legendary do not begin to describe it. It was not only about the music, but hope for a better world and the conviction that we young people would make it happen. It was a freer and more naive time.

The music at Woodstock was the flower of the flower of all the music which flowed from the Delta and Chicago blues, Motown and groundbreaking artists like Sister Rosetta Tharpe, Little Richard, Chuck Berry and other seminal black artists whose music had already evolved into early rock 'n roll. Then the white folk, blessed by the black, took up the banner of rock 'n roll as well. The best of all of these were the artists, white, brown and black, who played at Woodstock.

I was seventeen and in high school living just outside of Washington, D.C., where my Dad worked at policy level in the government and my Mom was active in the civil rights movement. They could not know that Woodstock would be the beginning of a life in music for me.

Woodstock, set on Max Yasgur's farm outside the town of Bethel, was a magnet and we felt its pull all the way down to Maryland. When I told my parents I wanted to go to Woodstock with my friend from study hall and her sister they said, ok, since she was clearly a responsible individual. After all, she had just been accepted into the first class at Yale which allowed women– and she had a driver's license already.

The music, uneven for a lot of reasons, was nevertheless an astounding jolt. It was a soundscape as lush as the rainforest and as fertile. The bands were some of the best and most creative in the era when rock 'n roll took hold of the planet. It used to be said the USA didn't need to send troops, just blue jeans and rock 'n roll and any evil regime would fall to democracy. Not so, but we wanted to believe it was. Again, it was a far more naive time.

If I had suspected before music was magic, this was confirmation: over 400,000 festival-goers agreed. After Woodstock, I was committed: I had to be inside music by playing it.

Woodstock was a phenomenon: not only was there a sublime cloud of music hovering over us all, but a community blossomed beneath it. If you talk with people who were there, meaning those who can remember anything from it due to their condition at the time, they will tell you it was unlike anything they experienced before or since.

My feeling is the same only I was sober the whole time so I actually can remember it all. This is my take on those three days in 1969

2

The Buzz and the Traffic

The Buzz

Our communication tools were primitive by today's standards. We had radio which was mostly AM, and newspapers, magazines and as always, word of mouth. The TV news, such as it was, had a field day with the very idea of so many hippies in one place. They had no idea how big this story would get.

The bright red posters for the festival were everywhere in the Washington, D.C., suburb where I lived. This was a little surprising since the festival was clearly advertising to rebellious young draft-dodgers, anti-war types, hippies and illegal drug takers. Yet there was not a lot of censorship. It was an openly contentious atmosphere.

Everyone I knew was talking about it, but few planned to go. I couldn't understand why not. Neither could my friends. I only recognized there would be Music. Great Music all weekend long.

I borrowed a sleeping bag and we set off with a tent, saucepan, some canned beans and $20. Although there have been many, many great adventures since, Woodstock remains one of the best of my life.

The Traffic Was Awful

It was a nightmare. Woodstock was 350 miles away and although we left at 7am and should have been there by noon but we didn't arrive until after 4pm.

Traffic was slowing by the time we got past Baltimore on our way up the coast. By the time we got to Pennsylvania and veered inland it was bumper-to-bumper. Then it slowed some more.

It was mid-August, the day was hot and the car had no ac. There were complete standstills of an hour and longer on all the roads within 100 miles from the festival site in Bethel. Later we learned the New State Thruway exits to the festival had been closed for hours and that we had just gotten through in time. We suffered sublime road weariness somehow laced with a numbed sense of excitement.

The spirit of the Festival began manifesting itself. The situation was exasperating but everyone on the road was good natured: no arguments, no fights. Drivers who tried to cut in front of other cars were soundly (but cheerfully and peacefully) booed. We'd all get there eventually.

People sat on cars and napped since the traffic was locked, or made friends with people in nearby cars. Some played guitars. Others ran off into the fields to find cover to relieve themselves–there were precious few filing stations with bathrooms en route. It was joyful madness. By the time we got to Woodstock we were a community.

Not everyone who wanted to go to the festival made it. Some said they were on their way, but gave up because of the traffic. Others said they got stoned in the spirit of solidarity, never made it out of the house and missed it all. A favorite story of not getting there was a kid aged about seven whose dad was an artist. His mom stopped the two of them right at the door and said, "You're taking him WHERE? O, no you don't." I did see even younger kids at Woodstock who were mostly naked, but happy, if a bit dirtier than usual. It seemed they were being well-taken care of by their parents.

When we finally arrived at the festival mid-afternoon we got as close as we could and parked alongside the country road. That was miles away and we walked in loaded with tent, etc. I slid off the hood of a car that gave me a ride and skinned my knee, but got it taken care of gratis once we camped. And it was already a party.

We had tickets, but most didn't. By now chicken wire gates to the festival were wide open, the fences were broken down and no one was taking tickets. People just walked in, trampling the fences. To the dismay of the organizers Michael Lang, Artie Kornfeld, Joel Rosenman and John P. Roberts, it had become a free festival.

3

Instant City

50,000 were expected but more just kept coming. By Friday evening some 400,000 were there. The Governor of New York State, Nelson Rockefeller, wanted to call in the National Guard, close the festival and evacuate everyone. But there was no riot to quell and the promoters talked him out of it, although Sullivan County did correctly declare a state of emergency. The festival continued.

Needless to say there was no seating chart. We camped up on the ridge just before the tree line where we could see and hear perfectly well, and get to the bathrooms water and food easily. When it rained the water ran downhill so we didn't have to deal much with the mud. We could play in it if we liked while others had to wallow.

Infrastructure—sorta

The light and speaker scaffolds were seven stories high. They stood like space age totems high above the field. The Hog Farm commune had been asked to help build these along with the stage and providing security and some food.

Other volunteers helped in the building, then helped themselves liberally to the champagne meant for the performers, including the man who later became one of my very distinguished teachers at Juilliard. He remembered clinging to the towers and drinking champagne from the bottle during a lightning storm. He said it was exhilarating, if stupid. Power to the People! As they say, youth is wasted on the young.

Concessions, What Concessions?

The few concessions in place were utterly unprepared for the gigantic crowd. Again, no one had expected hundreds of thousands: attendance was over 400,000, eight times the predictions of 50,000.

We had a meager few hamburger stands and a handful of other booths in the woods selling some food. There were spigots with running water all over, where you could get water free. But there were also locals selling Dixie cups of garden hose water for the outrageous sum of $.50 ($4.04 in today's money.) Those who had brought their own food shared it with strangers. It was a very generous gathering.

There were portable restrooms and I didn't smell sewage except around those. I am sure people used the woods, too. Surprisingly, people kept it together. Thank God.

The Hog Farm

The organizers had hired The Hog Farm commune to build the towers and stage and then help with communal kitchens and security. The commune quickly proved itself essential in managing the crowd's needs.

The task was enormous, but a member of the Hog Farm known as Wavy Gravy (Hugh Romney) shouldered it and became the de facto Mayor of Woodstock. Tirelessly making announcements at all hours about logistics, the multitudes of performance delays, warning about bad acid, reuniting lost kids with their parents, asking people to clear a path for medical volunteers, he soothed us and calm prevailed. He was responsible, competent and level-headed in a crazy situation, something not expected of a hippie.

Food Shortages

Food ran out very quickly and the roads to local grocery stores were impassable by car or on foot. So the legendary Hog Farm Kitchen went to work cooking brown rice and veggies for those who could get to their food tables near the woods and passed granola in Dixie cups around for those who stayed on their primo spots. If you left your coveted spot chances are either you would not find your way back to it or that someone would move into your vacant space, so a lot of people stayed where they were except for much-needed bathroom breaks.

We hadn't brought enough food either. Who knew we wouldn't be able to make it to the local food stores? I remember finding the Hog Farmers. Their food was free and healthy and they were nice. Everyone I encountered at Woodstock was polite. Several times while I wandered around taking it all in some stranger would pass me a plate of food. All for free, naturally. I would say "thanks" and they would smile.

Another friend insisted the Hog Farmers manning the food tables were naked and painted blue, not that he minded. I noticed no such thing. Like many he was very stoned. Since I wasn't, I trust my memory, not his. I ate their food many times and saw no naked blue people.

"Please Force" Security

Security was run by their "Please Force" as in "please don't do this, do this instead." Wavy Gravy said he intended to enforce peace with seltzer bottles and cream pies, as necessary. I guess it worked. I saw absolutely no fights, no arguments of any kind for the whole three days. I did learn how to curse after hearing the f*** word said so much.

Communications

What a logistical nightmare it was without telephones. Instead Wavy Gravy did yeoman work keeping us apprised of what was happening with his constant announcements over the pa system.

Runners and Angels

Tireless runners would thread their way through the crowd with urgent messages or small medical supplies and sometimes someone on a stretcher. The Hells Angels helped, too, by giving anyone who had to get out of the crowd a ride. They rode skillfully, carefully, quietly and were unfailingly polite. Of course, Altamont was a different story. At Woodstock we all got along.

Helicopters

Without helicopters it would have been a catastrophe. Supplying 400,000 people was an astounding feat of logistics. The helicopters never stopped landing and taking off.

The Sullivan County Sheriff's Department, realizing they couldn't arrest all 400,000 for drug possession (they gave up after 100 arrests) decided to help instead. They ordered in an Army helicopter and then distributed 10,000 sandwiches, along with blankets and medical supplies. At one point it dropped flowers on the crowd. And the farm owner, Max

Yasgur, helped unload the medical supplies delivered by helicopter.

After the first few hours performers couldn't get in or out by any kind of ground transportation. So they were flown back and forth by helicopter instead. In medical emergencies, people were flown out. The Hells Angels gave people rides to the 'copters. They were involved in some very black things at Altamont, but not at Woodstock. Here, they hadn't been hired; they were volunteering. The ones I came across were surprisingly polite and respectful to me–a gangling seventeen year old, and to everyone else as far as I could tell.

4

The Music

The musicians struggled to perform in intense summer heat, drenching rain, amidst electric shocks from ungrounded equipment and endured hours upon hours of delayed performances. Many ended up performing after waiting all night or all day. They were playing for an unprecedented number of people which sometimes amped up stage fright to an excruciating level. It was rough. But they still produced iconic performances.

By Friday evening we were all on Woodstock time: things happened when they could. Schedule, what schedule? Acts were rearranged constantly. True, there were a lot of drugs around, mostly grass, some hash, acid and mushrooms which did yield some delayed and/or lackluster performances, but there were many more memorable top notch performances than not.

Delays of up to five hours due to rain and technical problems had bands playing in the wee hours of the night or very, very early morning. So I didn't hear everyone. In fact, I missed Jimi Hendrix because I was still asleep when he finally got onstage to close the festival.

The Opening Act

On the first day of the festival, Friday afternoon at 2:30, the opening act was already three hours late. Richie Havens was supposed to go on fifth, but no one else had made it yet. Understand, cars were jammed for miles in all directions and no one could get through, including his entire band.

He took to the stage alone, terrified all these white people would throw things at him for being so late and so black; they didn't and he played a hastily improvised set for 50 minutes straight until someone else showed up. He swears it felt like three hours. And so, he opened Woodstock.

The influence of Indian music and spirituality created globally by the Beatles (yes, they were that influential) after their trip to India was felt at the festival. "The Woodstock Guru" Sri Swami Satchidananda, spoke to us awhile at the start of the festival about harmony and peace. I recall his presence was warm and his words seemed to be just for me. The interesting thing was everyone around me felt exactly the same way. It was an astounding brush with someone living on a higher plane. And no drugs were needed for that!

Together, he and Richie Havens showed us that the festival could be about peace with freedom, if we chose to make it so. And we heard them both, and we did.

George Harrison quietly attended Woodstock to support his guru and his sitar teachers. Harrison learned the basics of sitar and it blended into his music and crossed over into jazz and beyond.

There is so much to say about the festival's music that I can only tell you it made a lifelong impression on me and many others. The music, now over 50 years old, speaks eloquently for itself.

5

My Top 10 Favorite Performances

1.Jimi Hendrix

Sadly, at 9am I was exhausted and still asleep for this legendary guitarist and his groundbreaking "Star Spangled Banner." He still gets my top rating. A revolutionary guitarist and stunning virtuoso, like many artists, his was a vulnerable personality. His death at 27 from a heroin overdose in 1970 was a tragic loss to music. He may have been greatest rock instrumentalist of all time.

2.Carlos Santana

Santana, of Latino heritage, was a spectacular breakout star, a crossover from Latin music and creator of Latin Rock Fusion. His own brand of rock with Latin percussion (in a rock band?) lyrics in English and Spanish, and tasty licks with a Spanish flavor was uniquely his own. His debut album had not yet been released. He was amazed at the response he got at the festival, which catapulted him to the forefront of rock. At 75 Santana remains a humble and productive artist, known for supporting emerging musicians.

3.Richie Havens

He was one of a handful of black artists at Woodstock and, besides, he was nervous at the size of the crowd. He courageously improvised a solo set on the spot (not easy) and played for 50 minutes straight until another act showed up. His "Freedom" jam was glorious. He left the stage exhausted and relieved, saying of the audience, that they turned out to be just people. His performance had set the tone for the entire festival: freedom.

4.Joe Cocker

Joe Cocker was a Brit who had his own strange but mesmerizing body language onstage, with a voice that somehow conveyed gravel and velvet at the same time. He packed so much emotion into his music that every song was riveting. The high point was his cover of the Beatles "With A Little Help From My Friends." He was known to have an alcohol problem so this song was gut-wrenchingly poignant. It felt as though he had embraced the crowd and was singing to us all as his friends, and thanking us for our support. No performer lives for anything but intimate communication with his audience and Joe did it with 400,000 of us.

5.Ravi Shankar

It wasn't rock n roll at all; it was classical North Indian music. Ravi Shankar, a traditional virtuoso of the sitar, waited for hours for the rain to stop and decided to go ahead anyhow.

Northern Indian music is improvised along scales called ragas. Different times of day have their own ragas. So while he had been planning on an afternoon raga, at midnight he played night time raga instead. A raga performed at its own correct time of day has a profound effect. There are things in the West western music world we have not explored in depth, but we can feel them!

He was accompanied on the tabla (pitched drum that makes various percussive pitches) by Alla Rakha.

They improvised together for the entire set and ended with a fast exchange which wove together rhythmic brilliance and melodic interplay. I was amazed by the level of musicianship. Though the music was foreign to me I had never heard anything so powerful yet refined.

It turns out he didn't like hippies (undisciplined drug takers! wallowing in the mud like water buffalos!) but came anyhow, probably to expose the West to his music. The Beatles had just been to India and George Harrison showed up quietly to support his sitar teacher. BTW Nora Jones is Ravi Shankar's daughter.

6.Crosby, Stills Nash and Young

It was only their second gig and it was in the wee hours of the morning. They said later they were scared out of their minds. It didn't show. They were expressive and amazingly tight. What great craftsmanship. Their "Suite Judy Blue Eyes" and "Wooden Ships on Water" were my favorites. I played their music all through college.

7.The Who

One of the very tightest acts at Woodstock the British band's "My Generation" became the theme song for what was later called the Woodstock generation. In unabashed rebellion against the status quo and a lot more, they made their own fashion: Roger Daltry in curls acting the rock god in a chest-baring long fringed leather jacket, John Entwhistle and Keith Moon in T-shirts and Peter Townsend in a skinny white jumpsuit. As a band they weren't about to conform to ANYTHING including hippie fashion. Peter Townshend did windmills on his guitar, but also played edgy, evolved stabbing lead guitar solos.

What a wonderful band. It's great when cutting edge meets fame. They were big enough to demand being paid up front. Good for them.

8.Janis Joplin

Ah, Janis. At Woodstock Janis Joplin was another one of the few acts who were paid up front ($10,000, a fortune in those days.) The year before she had topped the Billboard charts, selling a million records of "Cheap Thrills."

This was the only time I saw her live and the recordings did not do justice to her sound or her sheer impact: she was a raw force of nature.

She had never played to a crowd that large (who had?) and was especially nervous. She had left her original band, Big Brother and the Holding Company, the year before and was feeling a bit insecure with her new top-notch band. She was under a lot of pressure. Nonetheless, I had never heard a musician give so much in a performance. Her "Piece of My Heart" left me speechless and I can feel its power even now, over 50 years later. The same goes for "Summertime" which was both raw and delicate and "Ball and Chain."

In performance she held nothing back and sang so loud she frayed her vocal cords. Genius singer that she was, she managed to use that to sing two notes at once.

Bigger than life, she died in 1970 of a heroin overdose at the age of 27, exactly like Jimi who passed the same way at the same age in the same year.

9.Country Joe and the Fish

This was a crowd -pleaser. Country Joe defrayed tension (we had been waiting for music for hours again) with his Fish Cheer. It went like this: give me an "F" and we roared back "F". Give me a "U." "U!" You see where this is going. "What does it spell?" And we all yelled that. "What does it spell?" We yelled and the collective frustration evaporated. Then he launched into "Feel Like I'm Going To Die Rag," an anti-war protest song. A note: that fall there was a global anti-Vietnam War protest of over 3 million people and 500,000 marched peacefully on the White House.

10.Jefferson Airplane

No Woodstock list is complete without the darlings of the subculture, the Jefferson Airplane. Grace Slick was their lead singer, a hippie culture goddess who looked and sounded the part. She dutifully turned in "White Rabbit," the hymn to mind-expanding drugs, but the band and she were exhausted. Then thrillingly, she rallied despite great fatigue, to produce a stellar rendition of "Volunteers of America," another anti-war song which showcased her voice with the band at the top of their abilities. Extremely impressive.

An Honorable Mention for The Grateful Dead

Jerry Garcia and his band got the short end of the stick due to severe thunderstorms and dangerous electrical equipment problems. A new ground wire had to be laid onstage because the rain, which had already kept them offstage for hours, had created a short which meant none of them could touch their instruments without getting a bad electric shock. Once that was straightened out the weary band played a very short, disorganized set before throwing in the towel. Who can blame them? It was a disappointment.

6

While Waiting Around...

People got creative while they were waiting for the next act. They found a swimming hole, roasted hot dogs, went through the Karma Wash, made music and made friends.

No, not everyone was naked. Full nudity occurred rarely, although not uncommonly among kids under six. A few people found aswimming hole and went skinny dipping. A photo which appeared in major magazines ledg many to believe the fair had been a sordid orgy of drugs and sex. But it wasn't.

It was the Summer of Free Love, and doubtless some people hooked up, but there was no public fornication– that I saw anyway.

At the Karma Wash, free of course, you walked through a double row of people waving colored fans and huge plumes of feathers at you. They were brushing your aura clean, they explained. And I actually felt lighter afterwards. Others said the same.

When the rains made mud, people played in it and had a good time, avoided it or put up with it.

7

Housing, Hygiene and Safety

Housing, what housing?

There were no structures built at the site for housing us. Some folks built their own lean-tos in the woods, others used vans or buses they'd managed to drive onto the ridge. Some of us had brought tents. Others had brought nothing and slept under the stars, yes, even in the rain. Somehow it worked out.

Hygiene, what hygiene?

Without showers on site and with roads still completely jammed, there was not a lot of washing. You could duck under one of the spigots on the site, go skinny dipping (I was too shy), or stand out in the rain but that was it. Festival-goers were not fundamentally dirty but had no access to shower water, just like any camping trip.

For all that, I didn't see or hear about anyone getting sick with the exception of one man, who said the Hog Farm food gave him dysentery, but this was the same one who saw blue people so I doubt it. I ate there frequently and never had any trouble.

Max Yasgur, owner of the farm, said the aftermath wasn't all that bad, though it sure looks like it from the day-after photos. He said he was pleased they cleaned up at all. Decades after archeologists working at the site (already? I thought that was for ancient civilizations) were frustrated with how little there was to dig up. The hippies had done too a good job of cleaning for that. Surprise.

Safety

Woodstock was surprisingly safe. An isolated act of violence was handled in typical Wavy Gravy fashion. Someone hungry and angry had burned down a hamburger stand one night. Gravy told us about it the next morning without reprimands or making any accusations, simply saying that a man's stand had burned down and asking, if we weren't too opposed to Capitalism, would we please help by buying the few hamburgers that were left?

There were two deaths from overdoses and one from a grisly tractor accident. There were also two births, a pretty good record for a roofless city with the population of Miami.

8

Dress, Undress and Festival Fashion

It is funny, but festival fashion now seems very, very similar to what we wore at Woodstock. Only we had imagined and made it ourselves by dreaming up an outfit then assembling its components. Tribal looks and other exotic styles were popular. Dressing in an Indian bedspread was great since you could twist it to make a dress, kaftan, skirt or scarf. Men and women both made bedspread clothes for themselves, no sewing involved. I saw a good amount of buckskin, most of it nicely done. It was all very individualistic and imaginative. I just wore shorts, sandals and a t-shirt the whole time. Full nudity occurred rarely, but not infrequently among kids under six.

9

Power to the People

Power to the People

In 1969 the People were those under 30 who wanted peace and maybe did some kind of drugs. They wore different clothes, had long hair and disapproved vehemently of the federal and state governments and capitalism. They felt they were the future and could change the world for the better.

But that mindset was fragile and lasted just a few years, quickly overwhelmed by working for a living, having a home, a marriage, kids and enjoying life as much as possible while doing all that. The People dried up and blew away. I miss the feeling that all was possible, and that the world, though misguided, was open to sweeping and positive change.

10

Beyond "Sex, Drugs and Rock 'n Roll"

It was probably the LSD Guru, Timothy Leary, who coined the phrase in a Playboy interview in the early '60's. It famously described a vibrant counter/subculture of young restless Americans. There were some public kisses and quite a few embraces. Maybe more was going on in the woods and in tents and other make-do shelters. But it was by no means a drug den or an orgy. And there was precious little nudity or public fornication. Again, not that I saw.

Underground Bureau of Standards

Drugs were indeed taken at Woodstock. There was weed, acid, hash, and some cocaine. Harder stuff was unusual. Warnings about bad acid or pot laced with speed saved a lot of people from getting sick or worse. So the public was protected, not by the FDA, but by Wavy Gravy and his runners who saw and reported it all. But it wasn't at all the outdoor drug den some (mostly those who weren't there) claimed.

When the Music Was More Than Enough

The music was a staggering amount of emotion and sensory input to

25

absorb. I was drawn into a vortex of sound, amplified by the energy of the thousands and thousands around me.

As a Performer, if you are doing it right, a circuit of energy (for lack of a more scientific term) is created when you play for a live audience. Sometimes it is almost palpable, and as an audience member, you have felt it, too. It gets stronger when there are more people listening. So you can imagine what that was like with the equivalent of an entire city listening and reacting. That was plenty for me and probably for many.

I didn't bother whenever someone offered me a joint, which happened a bunch of times. I was already busy—listening and watching it all. It would have been nice to have some champagne but we didn't find any. By the way, I definitely wasn't the only sober one there. Not everyone seemed stoned by a long shot. The music was that powerful.

11

The Peaceful Clan

At Woodstock we were a self-selected group of mostly young mostly white people attracted by the music and the prospect of three days of freedom from regular life. The very few black or Latino people were welcomed with no issues.

The conditions at the fair were uncomfortable at times, but not terrible: a long congested trip to the fairgrounds was followed by thronged conditions with little sleep unless you wanted to miss all the insanely rearranged acts. We didn't get fat but we didn't starve either. There was rain, some mud, well, depending on where you were seated maybe a lot of mud, and for performers and audience alike hours and hours of delays. Still everyone remained mellow and helpful to one another. The opening theme of peace with freedom prevailed all the way through the festival. It just seemed normal.

Truly going with the flow, people were happy, friendly and not prone to argue with their circumstances. For some people, it was clearly the freest they'd ever felt or ever would feel. If some part of that was due to drugs it was still mighty impressive.

12

Conclusion

I look at Woodstock as more of a possibility than an event. For me it remains unique and magical. What a privilege to be at the heart of the music of that time. So much came out of that era.

Even more significant for me was the experience of so many people being kind to one another for no reason. It is possible. And the joy. The simple joy of being alive together.

Thank you for traveling there with me. If you enjoyed it, please leave a favorable review of my book.

13

Resources

https://www.mic.com/articles/136969/who-invented-rock-n-roll-these-are-the-black-pioneers-who-laid-the-genre-s-foundations

https://en.wikipedia.org/wiki/Woodstock

https://stacker.com/stories/2583/how-well-do-you-remember-1969#:~:text=Of%20course%2C%20the%20most%20famous%20event,Buzz%20Aldrin%20followed%2019%20minutes%20later.&text=Of%20course%2C%20the%20most,followed%2019%20minutes%20later.&text=the%20most%20famous%20event,Buzz%20Aldrin%20followed%2019

https://www.verywellhealth.com/a-brief-history-on-the-birth-control-pill-3522634

https://en.wikipedia.org/wiki/Timeline_of_the_Richard_Nixon_presidency_(1969)

RESOURCES

https://www.history.com/topics/gay-rights/the-stonewall-riots

https://www.bing.com/search?q=first+episode+of+monty+python&qs=SC&pq=first+episdoe+of+of+monty+python&sc=1-32&cvid=9B6DECF32C2E4EBF859A16B7A0BBB982&FORM=QBRE&sp=1

https://stockinvesting.today/ma1607/article/the-1969-bear-market?

https://rarehistoricalphotos.com/woodstock-pictures-1969/

https://en.wikipedia.org/wiki/Hog_Farm

https://www.bing.com/search?q=organizers%20of%20hte%20woodstock%20festival&FORM=ARPSEC&PC=ARPL&PTAG=30039

https://www.huffpost.com/entry/food-at-woodstock_n_6793300

https://www.bethelwoodscenter.org/blog/janis-joplinHOusing

https://www.rollingstone.com/music/music-features/woodstock-richie-havens-855505/

https://pophistorydig.com/topics/tag/janis-joplin-at-woodstock/

https://vak1969.com/2018/09/08/50th-anniversary-of-1969-the-greatest-year-of-the-century/

https://ultimateclassicrock.com/woodstock-performances/

Epilogue

"What is proved was once only imagined." —-William Blake

www.ingramcontent.com/pod-product-compliance
Lightning Source LLC
Chambersburg PA
CBHW051408150726

48000CB00003B/1376